CONGREGATION FOR T

INSTRUCTION

THE PASTORAL CONVERSION OF THE PARISH COMMUNITY

in the Service of the Evangelising Mission of the Church

*All documents are published
thanks to the generosity of the supporters
of the Catholic Truth Society*

This edition first published 2020 by The Incorporated Catholic Truth Society 42-46 Harleyford Road London SE11 5AY.

ISBN 978 1 78469 644 3

CONTENTS

INTRODUCTION

1. The ecclesiological reflection of the Second Vatican Council, together with the considerable social and cultural changes of recent decades, has resulted in various Particular Churches having to reorganise the manner in which the pastoral care of Parish communities are assigned. This has made it possible to initiate new experiences, enhancing the dimension of communion and implementing, under the guidance of pastors, a harmonious synthesis of charisms and vocations at the service of the proclamation of the Gospel, which better corresponds to the demands of evangelisation today.

Pope Francis, at the beginning of his Petrine ministry, recalled the importance of "creativity", meaning thereby "seeking new ways", that is "seeking how best to proclaim the Gospel"; in respect of this, the Holy Father concluded by saying, "the Church, and also the Code of Canon Law, gives us innumerable possibilities, much freedom to seek these things"[1].

2. The situations outlined in the following Instruction represent a valuable opportunity for pastoral conversion that is essentially missionary. Parish communities will find herein a call to go out of themselves, offering instruments for reform, even structural, in a spirit of communion and collaboration, of encounter and closeness, of mercy and solicitude for the proclamation of the Gospel.

---

[1] Francis, Discussion with Parish Priests of Rome (16th September 2013): *http://cosarestadelgiorno.wordpress.com/2013/09/16/*

I. PASTORAL CONVERSION

3. Pastoral conversion is one of the central themes in the "new phase of evangelisation"[2] that the Church is called to foster today, whereby Christian communities be ever more centres conducive to an encounter with Christ.

The Holy Father, in this regard, recommends that: "If something should rightly disturb us and trouble our consciences, it is the fact that so many of our brothers and sisters are living without the strength, light and consolation born of friendship with Jesus Christ, without a community of faith to support them, without meaning and a goal in life. More than by fear of going astray, my hope is that we will be moved by the fear of remaining shut up within structures which give us a false sense of security, within rules which make us harsh judges, within habits which make us feel safe, while at our door people are starving and Jesus does not tire of saying to us: 'Give them something to eat' (*Mk* 6:37)"[3].

4. Urged on by this concern, the Church "faithful to her own tradition and at the same time conscious of her universal mission, she can enter into communion with the various civilisations, to their enrichment and the enrichment of the Church herself"[4]. The fruitful and creative encounter between the Gospel and the culture leads to true progress: on the one hand, the Word of God is incarnate in the history of men, thus renews it; on the other hand, "the Church [...] can and ought to be enriched by the development of human social life"[5], enhancing thereby, in our present age, the mission entrusted to her by Christ.

---

[2] Cf. Id., Apostolic Exhortation *Evangelii gaudium* (24th November 2013), n. 287: AAS 105 (2013), 1136.

[3] Ibid., n. 49: AAS 105 (2013), 1040.

[4] Second Vatican Ecumenical Council, Pastoral constitution on the Church in the modern world *Gaudium et spes* (7th December 1965), n. 58: AAS 58 (1966), 1079.

[5] Ibid., n. 44: AAS 58 (1966), 1065.

5. The Church proclaims that the Word "became flesh and lived among us" (*Jn* 1:14). This Word of God, who loves to dwell in our midst, in his inexhaustible richness[6], was received the world over by diverse peoples, inspiring in them the most noble of aspirations, such as the desire for God, the dignity of every human life, equality among men and respect for difference within the single human family, dialogue as a means to participation, a longing for peace, welcome as an expression of fraternity and solidarity, together with a responsible care for creation[7].

It is unthinkable, therefore, that such newness, whose propagation to the ends of the earth remains incomplete, abates or, worse still, disappears[8]. In order for the journey of the Word to continue, the Christian community must make a determined missionary decision "capable of transforming everything, so that the Church's customs, ways of doing things, times and schedules, language and structures can be suitably channelled for the evangelisation of today's world rather than for her self-preservation"[9].

---

[6] Cf. Saint Ephrem, *Commentary on Tatian's Diatessaron* 1, 18-19: SC 121, 52-53.

[7] Francis, Encyclical Letter *Laudato sì* (24th May 2015), n. 68: AAS 107 (2015), 847.

[8] Cf. Paul VI, Encyclical Letter *Ecclesiam suam* (6th August 1964): AAS 56 (1964), 639.

[9] *Evangelii gaudium*, n. 27: AAS 105 (2013), 1031.

II. THE PARISH IN A CONTEMPORARY CONTEXT

6. The aforesaid missionary conversion, which naturally leads to a reform of structures, concerns the Parish in particular, namely that community gathered around the Table of the Word and the Eucharist.

The Parish has a long history and, from the outset, it has played a fundamental role in the life of Christians and in the development and pastoral work of the Church. We can see this in the writings of Saint Paul. Several of the Pauline texts show us the formation of small communities as domestic churches, which the Apostle simply calls a "house" (cf., for example, *Rm* 16:3-5; *1 Co* 16:19-20; *Phil* 4:22). With these "houses", we get a foretaste of the birth of the first "Parishes".

7. Since its inception, the Parish is envisioned as a response to a precise pastoral need, namely that of bringing the Gospel to the People through the proclamation of the faith and the celebration of the Sacraments. The etymology of the word makes clear the meaning of the institution: the Parish is a house among houses[10] and is a response to the logic of the Incarnation of Jesus Christ, alive and active among the community. It is visibly characterised then, as a place of worship, a sign of the permanent presence of the Risen Lord in the midst of his People.

8. The territorial configuration of the Parish, however, must confront a peculiar characteristic of our contemporary world, whereby increased mobility and the digital culture have expanded the confines of existence. On the one hand, people are less associated today with a definite and immutable geographical context, living instead in "a global and pluralist village"; on the other hand, the digital culture has inevitably altered the concept

---

[10] Cf. John Paul II, Post-Synodal Apostolic Exhortation *Christifideles laici* (30th December 1988), n. 26: AAS 81 (1989), 438.

of space, together with people's language and behaviour, especially in younger generations.

Moreover, it is quite easy to hypothesise about how the continuous development of technology will ultimately change our way of thinking, together with the understanding of self and of social living. The speed of change, successive cultural models, the ease of movement and the speed of communication are transforming the perception of space and time.

9. As a living community of believers, the Parish finds itself in a context whereby the territorial affiliation is increasingly less evident, where places of association are multiplied and where interpersonal relationships risk being dissolved into a virtual world without any commitment or responsibility towards one's neighbour.

10. It is noteworthy how such cultural changes and the evolving territorial ties are fostering within the Church, through the grace of the Holy Spirit, a new discernment around community, "which consists in seeing reality with the eyes of God, with a view to unity and communion"[11]. The whole People of God must urgently embrace the Holy Spirit's invitation to begin the process of "renewing" the face of the Church.

---

[11] Francis, General Audience (12th June 2019): *L'Osservatore Romano* 134 (13th June 2019), 1.

III. THE VALUE OF THE PARISH TODAY

11. In virtue of this discernment, the Parish is called upon to read the signs of the times, while adapting both to the needs of the faithful and to historical changes. A renewed vitality is required that favours the rediscovery of the vocation of the baptised as a disciple of Jesus Christ and a missionary of the Gospel, in light of the Second Vatican Council and subsequent Magisterium.

12. The Council Fathers were prescient in writing: "the care of souls should always be infused with a missionary spirit"[12]. In continuity with this teaching, Saint John Paul II specified that: "Whilst the Parish is perfected and integrated in a variety of forms, it nevertheless remains an indispensable organism of primary importance in the visible structure of the Church", whereby "evangelisation is the cornerstone of all pastoral action, the demands of which are primary, pre-eminent and preferential"[13]. Subsequently, Benedict XVI taught, "the parish is a beacon that radiates the light of the faith and thus responds to the deepest and truest desires of the human heart, giving meaning and hope to the lives of individuals and families"[14]. Lastly, Pope Francis recalled how "the parish encourages and trains its members to be evangelisers"[15].

13. In order to promote the centrality of the missionary presence of the Christian community in the world[16], it is important not only to think about a new experience of Parish, but also about

---

[12] Second Vatican Ecumenical Council, Decree on the Pastoral Office of Bishops in the Church *Christus Dominus* (28th October 1965), n. 30: AAS 58 (1966), 688.

[13] John Paul II, Discourse to Participants at the Plenary of the Congregation for the Clergy (20th October 1984), ns. 3 and 4: Insegnamenti VII/2 (1984), 984 and 985; cf. also Id., Apostolic Exhortation *Catechesi tradendae* (16th October 1979), n. 67: AAS 71 (1979), 1332.

[14] Benedict XVI, Homily during the pastoral visit to Our Lady Star of Evangelisation Parish of Rome (10th December 2006): Insegnamenti II/2 (2006), 795.

[15] *Evangelii gaudium*, n. 28: AAS 105 (2013) 1032.

[16] Cf. *Gaudium et spes*, n. 4: AAS 58 (1966), 1027.

the ministry and mission of priests, who, together with the lay faithful, have the task of being "salt and light of the world" (cf. *Mt* 5:13-14), a "lamp on a lampstand" (cf. *Mk* 4:21), showing forth the face of an evangelising community, capable of an adequate reading of the signs of the times and of giving witness to coherent evangelical living.

14. Beginning with a consideration of the signs of the times, it is necessary, in listening to the Spirit, to produce new signs. With the Parish no longer being the primary gathering and social centre, as in former days, it is thus necessary to find new forms of accompaniment and closeness. A task of this kind ought not to be seen as a burden, but rather as a challenge to be embraced with enthusiasm.

15. Imitating their Master, the Lord's disciples, in the school of saints and shepherds, learned, not without suffering, how to await the times and ways of God, thus nurturing the certainty that he is present until the end of time, and that the Holy Spirit – the beating heart in the life of the Church– gathers together the children of God dispersed throughout the world. As a result, the Christian community should not be afraid to begin and accompany processes within territories that are host to diverse cultures, in the sure and certain hope that, for the disciples of Christ, "nothing genuinely human fails to raise an echo in their hearts"[17].

---

[17] Cf. *Gaudium et spes*, n. 1: AAS 58 (1966), 1025-1026.

IV. MISSION: THE GUIDING PRINCIPLE FOR RENEWAL

16. Given the above-mentioned changing realities, their generous dedication notwithstanding, the current Parish model no longer adequately corresponds to the many expectations of the faithful, especially when one considers the multiplicity of community types in existence today[18]. It is true that a characteristic of the Parish is its rootedness at the centre of where people live from day to day. However, the Parish territory is no longer a geographical space only, but also the context in which people express their lives in terms of relationships, reciprocal service and ancient traditions. It is in this "existential territory" where the challenges facing the Church in the midst of the community are played out. As a result, any pastoral action that is limited to the territory of the Parish is outdated, which is something the parishioners themselves observe when their Parish appears to be more interested in preserving a nostalgia of former times as opposed to looking to the future with courage[19]. It is worth noting, however, that from a canonical perspective, the territorial principle remains in force, when required by law[20].

17. Moreover, mere repetitive action that fails to have an impact upon people's concrete lives remains a sterile attempt at survival, which is usually welcomed by general indifference. If the Parish does not exude that spiritual dynamic of evangelisation, it runs the risk of becoming self-referential and fossilised, offering

---

[18] Cf. *Evangelii gaudium*, ns. 72-73: AAS 105 (2013), 1050-1051

[19] Cf. Synod of Bishops, XV Ordinary General Assembly (3rd-28th October 2018): "Young people, the faith and vocational discernment", Final Document, n. 129 "In this context, an understanding of the parish defined solely by territorial borders and incapable of engaging the faithful in a wide range of initiatives, especially the young, would imprison the parish in unacceptable stagnation and in worryingly repetitive pastoral cycles": *L'Osservatore Romano* 247 (29th-30th October 2018), 10.

[20] Cf. for example, C.I.C., cann. 102; 1015-1016; 1108, §1.

experiences that are devoid of evangelical flavour and missionary drive, of interest only to small groups.

18. The renewal of evangelisation requires a new approach with diverse pastoral proposals, so that the Word of God and the sacramental life can reach everyone in a way that is coherent with their state in life. Ecclesial membership in our present age is less a question of birthplace, much less where someone grew up, as it is about being part of a community by adoption[21], where the faithful have a more extensive experience of the Word of God than they do of being a body made up of many members, with everyone working for the common good (*1 Co* 12:12-27).

19. Over and above places and reasons for membership, the Parish community is the human context wherein the evangelising work of the Church is carried out, where Sacraments are celebrated and where charity is exercised, all with missionary zeal, which, apart from being an intrinsic part of pastoral action, is a litmus test of its authenticity. In this present age, marked at times by marginalisation and solitude, the Parish community is called to be a living sign of the proximity of Christ through fraternal bonds, ever attentive to new forms of poverty.

20. In view of what has been said so far, it is necessary to identify perspectives that allow for the renewal of "traditional" Parish structures in terms of mission. This is the heart of the desired pastoral conversion, which must touch the proclamation of the Word of God, the sacramental life and the witness of charity, in other words the essential areas in which the Parish grows and conforms to the Mystery in which it believes.

21. Perusing the Acts of the Apostles, one realises the transformative effect of the Word of God, that interior power that brings about the conversion of hearts. The Word is the food that nourishes the Lord's disciples and makes them witnesses to the Gospel in the various circumstances of life. The Scriptures

---

[21] *Christifideles laici*, n. 25: AAS 81 (1989), 436-437.

contain a prophetic impetus that makes them into a living force. It is necessary to provide instruction on how to listen and meditate on the Word of God through a variety of different approaches to proclamation[22], adopting clear and comprehensible means of communication that announce the Lord Jesus according to the ever new witness of the kerygma[23].

22. The celebration of the Eucharistic mystery is "the source and summit of the whole Christian life"[24] and accordingly, the essential moment for building up the Parish community. Therein, the Church becomes aware of the meaning of her name (*ecclesia*): the coming together of the People of God to praise, implore, intercede and give thanks. In celebrating the Eucharist, the Christian community welcomes the living presence of the Crucified and Risen Lord, receiving the announcement of the entire mystery of salvation.

23. The Church perceives here the need to rediscover Christian initiation, which generates new life, as it is placed within the mystery of God's own life. It is a journey that is ongoing, that transcends celebrations or events, because, in essence, it is defined, not as a duty to fulfil a "rite of passage", but rather as a perpetual *sequela Christi*. In this context, it would be useful to establish a mystagogical itinerary that genuinely affects existence[25]. Catechesis needs to be presented as an ongoing proclamation of the Mystery of Christ, the objective of which is to foster in the heart of the baptised that full stature of Christ (cf. *Eph* 4:13) that is derived from a personal encounter with the Lord of life.

Pope Francis has recalled the need to "mention two false forms of holiness that can lead us astray: gnosticism and pelagianism. They are two heresies from early Christian times, yet they

---

[22] Cf. *Evangelii gaudium*, n. 174: AAS 105 (2013), 1093.

[23] Cf. ibid., n. 164-165: AAS 105 (2013), 1088-1089.

[24] Second Vatican Ecumenical Council, Dogmatic Constitution on the Church *Lumen gentium* (21st November 1964), n. 11: AAS 57 (1965), 15.

[25] Cf. *Evangelii gaudium*, ns. 166-167: AAS 105 (2013), 1089-1090.

continue to plague us"[26]. In the case of gnosticism, one is dealing with an abstract faith that is purely intellectual and made up of knowledge that is far from lived reality; meanwhile, pelagianism leads man to depend on his own abilities, thus ignoring the action of the Holy Spirit.

24. In the mysterious interplay between the action of God and that of man, the proclamation of the Gospel comes through men and women who give credibility to what they say through the witness of their lives, together with their interpersonal relationships that inspire trust and hope. In these times, marked as they are by indifferentism, individualism and the exclusion of others, the rediscovery of brotherhood is paramount and integral to evangelisation, which is closely linked to human relationships[27]. In this way, the Christian community makes Our Lord's words their own, as they spur us to "put out into the deep" (*Lk* 5:4), trusting in the Master as we pay out the nets in the assurance of hauling a "large catch"[28].

25. The "culture of encounter" is conducive to dialogue, solidarity and openness to others, as it is person-centred. Naturally, a Parish must be a place that brings people together and fosters long-term personal relationships, thereby giving people a sense of belonging and being wanted.

---

[26] Francis, Apostolic Exhortation on the call to holiness in the contemporary world *Gaudete et exsultate* (19th March 2018), n. 35: AAS 110 (2018), 1120. The following words of Pope Francis with regard gnosticism and pelagianism are also worth recalling here: "This worldliness can be fuelled in two deeply interrelated ways. One is the attraction of gnosticism, a purely subjective faith whose only interest is a certain experience or a set of ideas and bits of information which are meant to console and enlighten, but which ultimately keep one imprisoned in his or her own thoughts and feelings. The other is the self-absorbed promethean neopelagianism of those who ultimately trust only in their own powers and feel superior to others because they observe certain rules or remain intransigently faithful to a particular Catholic style from the past". *Evangelii gaudium*, n. 94: AAS 105 (2013), 1059-1060; cf. also Congregation for the Doctrine of the Faith, Letter *Placuit Deo* (22nd February 2018): AAS 110 (2018), 429.

[27] Cf. *Letter to Diognetus* V, 1-10: Patres Apostolici, ed. F.X. Funk, vol. 1, Tubingae 1901, 398.

[28] Cf. John Paul II, Apostolic Letter *Novo millennio ineunte* (6th January 2001), n. 1: AAS 93 (2001), 266.

26. The Parish community is called truly to master the "art of accompaniment". If deep roots are planted, the Parish will become a place where solitude is overcome, which has affected so many lives, as well as being "a sanctuary where the thirsty come to drink in the midst of their journey and a centre of constant missionary outreach"[29].

---

[29] *Evangelii gaudium*, n. 28: AAS 105 (2013), 1032.

V. "A COMMUNITY OF COMMUNITIES": A PARISH THAT IS INCLUSIVE, EVANGELISING AND ATTENTIVE TO THE POOR

27. The subject of the missionary and evangelising action of the Church is always the People of God as a whole. The Code of Canon Law emphasises that the Parish is not identified as a building or a series of structures, but rather as a specific community of the faithful, where the Parish Priest is the proper pastor[30]. Pope Francis recalled that "the parish is the presence of the Church in a given territory, an environment for hearing God's word, for growth in the Christian life, for dialogue, proclamation, charitable outreach, worship and celebration", and affirmed that it is "a community of communities"[31].

28. The various components that make up the Parish are called to communion and unity. When each part recognises its complementary role in service of the community, on the one hand, we see the fulfilment of the collaborative ministry of the Parish Priest with his Assistant Priests, while on the other hand, we see how the various charisms of deacons, consecrated men and women and the laity co-operate in building up the singular body of Christ (cf. *1 Co* 12:12).

29. The Parish is a community gathered together by the Holy Spirit to announce the Word of God and bring new children of God to birth in the baptismal font. Assembled by the pastor, the Parish celebrates the memorial of the passion, death and resurrection of the Lord, bearing witness to faith in charity, living in a permanent state of mission, whilst ensuring that no one is excluded from the salvific, life-giving message. Pope Francis

---

[30] Cf. C.I.C. cann. 515; 518; 519.

[31] *Evangelii gaudium*, n. 28: AAS 105 (2013), 1031-1032.

expressed it thus: "The parish is not an outdated institution; precisely because it possesses great flexibility, it can assume quite different contours depending on the openness and missionary creativity of the pastor and the community. While certainly not the only institution which evangelises, if the parish proves capable of self-renewal and constant adaptability, it continues to be 'the Church living in the midst of the homes of her sons and daughters'. This presumes that it really is in contact with the homes and the lives of its people, and does not become a useless structure out of touch with people or a self-absorbed group made up of a chosen few. [...] We must admit, though, that the call to review and renew our parishes has not yet sufficed to bring them nearer to people, to make them environments of living communion and participation, and to make them completely mission-oriented"[32].

30. The "spiritual and ecclesial style of Shrines" – which are true "missionary outposts" in their own right – is not extraneous to the Parish, characterised as they are by their sprit of welcome, their life of prayer and silence that renews the spirit, the celebration of the Sacrament of Reconciliation and their care for the poor. Parish pilgrimages to various Shrines are precious instruments that can serve to strengthen fraternal communion, openness and welcome upon return to the Parish[33].

31. A Shrine, then, is analogous to a Parish in that it encompasses all the characteristics and services that ought to be found in the parish community, as it represents for the faithful the desired goal of their interior searching and a place where they can encounter the merciful face of Christ in a welcoming Church.

Frequenting Shrines can help the faithful rediscover their being "anointed by the Holy One" (*1 Jn* 2:20), that is to say their baptismal consecration. At such places, one learns to celebrate

---

[32] *Evangelii gaudium*, n. 28: AAS 105 (2013), 1031-1032.

[33] Cf. Francis, Post-Synodal Apostolic Exhortation *Christus vivit* (25th March 2019), n. 238, Vatican City 2019.

with fervour the mysterious presence of God in the midst of his people in the liturgy, in the beauty of the evangelising mission of the baptised, and in the call to exercise charity in daily life[34].

32. A "sanctuary" open to all, the Parish, called to reach out to everyone, without exception, should remember that the poor and excluded must always have a privileged place in the heart of the Church. As Pope Benedict XVI affirmed: "The Gospel is addressed in a special way to the poor"[35]. In addition, as Pope Francis observed "the new evangelisation is an invitation to acknowledge the saving power at work in their lives and to put them at the centre of the Church's pilgrim way. We are called to find Christ in them, to lend our voice to their causes, but also to be their friends, to listen to them, to speak for them and to embrace the mysterious wisdom which God wishes to share with us through them"[36].

33. Often, the Parish community is the first place of personal human encounter that the poor have with the face of the Church. Priests, deacons and consecrated men and women are among the first to have compassion for the "wounded flesh"[37] of their brothers and sisters, to visit the sick, to support the unemployed and their families, thereby opening the door to those in need. With their gaze fixed upon them, the Parish community evangelises and is evangelised by the poor, discovering anew the call to preach the Word in all settings[38], whilst recalling the "supreme law" of charity, by which we shall all be judged[39].

---

[34] Cf. Id., Bull of Indiction *Misericordiae vultus* (11th April 2015), n. 3: AAS 107 (2015), 400-401.

[35] Benedict XVI, Address to the Bishops of Brazil (11th May 2007), n. 3: Insegnamenti III/I (2007), 826.

[36] *Evangelii gaudium*, n. 198: AAS 105 (2013), 1103.

[37] Cf. Francis, Morning Meditation at Santa Marta (30th October 2017).

[38] Cf. *Evangelii gaudium*, ns. 186-216: AAS 105 (2013), 1098-1109.

[39] Cf. *Gaudete et exsultate*, ns. 95-99: AAS 110 (2018), 1137-1138.

VI. FROM THE CONVERSION OF PEOPLE TO THAT OF STRUCTURES

34. In the process of renewal and restructuring, the Parish has to avoid the risk of falling into an excessive and bureaucratic organisation of events and an offering of services that do not express the dynamic of evangelisation, but rather the criterion of self-preservation[40].

Quoting Saint Paul VI, Pope Francis, with his usual *parrhesia*, stated: "The Church must look with penetrating eyes within herself, ponder the mystery of her own being (...) There are ecclesial structures which can hamper efforts at evangelisation, yet even good structures are only helpful when there is a life constantly driving, sustaining and assessing them. Without new life and an authentic evangelical spirit, without the Church's 'fidelity to her own calling', any new structure will soon prove ineffective"[41].

35. The conversion of structures, which the Church must undertake, requires a significant change in mentality and an interior renewal, especially among those entrusted with the responsibility of pastoral leadership. In order to remain faithful to the mandate of Christ, pastors, especially Parish Priests who "are co-workers of the bishop in a very special way"[42], must resolutely grasp the need for a missionary reform of pastoral action.

36. Taking into consideration the profound emotional and nostalgic bonds within a Christian community, pastors ought not to forget that the faith of the People of God is interwoven

---

[40] Cf. *Evangelii gaudium*, n. 27: AAS 105 (2013), 1031; cf. also ibid., n. 189: AAS 105 (2013), 1099: "Changing structures without generating new convictions and attitudes will only ensure that those same structures will become, sooner or later, corrupt, oppressive and ineffectual".

[41] Ibid., n. 26: AAS 105 (2013), 1030-1031.

[42] *Christus Dominus*, n. 30: AAS 58 (1966), 688.

with familial and communal memories. Often, a sacred place can evoke important milestones in the life of past generations, where faces and occasions have influenced personal and familial journeys. In order to avoid trauma and hurt in the process of restructuring a Parish or, at times, diocesan communities, it is imperative that it be carried out with flexibility and gradualism.

In reference to the reform of the Roman Curia, Pope Francis emphasised that gradualism "has to do with the necessary discernment entailed by historical processes, the passage of time and stages of development, assessment, correction, experimentation, and approvals *ad experimentum.* In these cases, it is not a matter of indecisiveness, but of the flexibility needed to be able to achieve a true reform"[43]. Accordingly, one should not act "hastily" in an attempt, as it were, to bring about immediate reforms by means of generic criteria that obey a "rational decision" to the detriment of those who actually live within the territory. Every plan must be situated within the lived experience of a community and implanted in it without causing harm, with a necessary phase of prior consultation, and of progressive implementation and verification.

37. Naturally, a renewal of this sort is not the responsibility solely of the Parish Priest, nor should it be imposed from above in such a way as to exclude the People of God. The pastoral conversion of structures implies the understanding that "the faithful Holy People of God are anointed with the grace of the Holy Spirit; therefore when we reflect, think, evaluate, discern, we must be very attentive to this anointing. Whenever as a Church, as pastors, as consecrated persons, we have forgotten this certainty, we have lost our way. Whenever we try to supplant, silence, look down on, ignore or reduce into small elites the People of God in their totality and differences, we construct communities, pastoral plans, theological accentuations, spiritualities, structures without

---

[43] Francis, *Presentation of Christmas Greetings to the Roman Curia* (22nd December 2016): AAS 109 (2017), 44.

roots, without history, without faces, without memory, without a body, in the end, without lives. To remove ourselves from the life of the People of God hastens us to the desolation and to a perversion of ecclesial nature"[44].

It does not pertain to the clergy alone, therefore, to carry out the transformation inspired by the Holy Spirit, since this involves the entire People of God[45]. It is necessary, however, "consciously and lucidly to seek areas of communion and participation so that the anointing of the People of God may find its concrete mediations to express itself"[46].

38. Consequently, the need to overcome a self-referential conception of the Parish or the "clericalisation of pastoral activity" becomes apparent. When it is acknowledged that the state of the People of God "is that of the dignity and freedom of the children of God, in whose hearts the Holy Spirit dwells as in his temple"[47], this inspires practices and models by which all the baptised, by virtue of the gift of the Holy Spirit and their infused charisms, become active participants of evangelisation, in the style and modality of an organic community, together with other Parish communities or at the diocesan level. In effect, the whole community, and not simply the hierarchy, is the responsible agent of mission, since the Church is identified as the entire People of God.

39. Pastors have the task of keeping this dynamic alive, so that the baptised realise that they are protagonists of evangelisation. The presbyterate, whose formation is ongoing[48], must exercise the art

---

[44] Id., Carta al Pueblo de Diós que peregrina en Chile (31st May 2018): *www.vatican. va/content/francesco/es/letters/2018/documents/papa-francesco_20180531_lettera-popolodidio-cile.html*

[45] Cf. ibid.

[46] Ibid.

[47] *Lumen gentium*, n. 9: AAS 57 (1965), 13.

[48] Cf. Congregation for the Clergy, *Ratio fundamentalis institutionis sacerdotalis* (8th December 2016), ns. 80-88, Vatican City 2016, pp. 37-42.

of discernment with prudence, in such a way as to allow the life of the Parish, with its diversity of vocations and ministries, to grow and mature. As a member and servant of the People of God entrusted to his care, the Priest cannot supplant this discernment. The Parish community has the ability to propose forms of ministry, to proclaim the faith and to bear witness to charity.

40. The centrality of the Holy Spirit – a free gift from the Father and the Son to the Church – profoundly enlivens the aspect of generosity, in accord with the teaching of Jesus, who said: "You received without charge, give without charge" (*Mk* 10:8). The Lord taught his disciples to have a generous spirit of service, to be a reciprocal gift for the other (cf. *Jn* 13:14-15), and to have a special care for the poor. From this derives the need not to "commercialise" the sacramental life, and not to give the impression that the celebration of the Sacraments, especially the Holy Eucharist, along with other ministerial activities, are subject to tariffs.

The pastor who willingly serves his flock with generosity, must instruct the faithful, however, in such a way that each member of the community feels responsible and directly involved in caring for the needs of the Church in a variety of ways and in a spirit of solidarity, which the Church requires in order to carry out her pastoral service with freedom and efficacy.

41. The mission required of the Parish, as a central driving force of evangelisation, concerns the People of God in its entirety: priests, deacons, consecrated men and women, and the lay faithful, each according to their respective charisms and the responsibility that corresponds to them.

VII. THE PARISH AND OTHER SUBDIVISIONS WITHIN THE DIOCESE

42. The pastoral conversion of the Parish community, in terms of mission, takes shape and finds expression in a gradual process of a renewal of structures; consequently, different forms of shared pastoral care emerge, as well as forms of participation in it that involve the entire People of God.

43. Using language borrowed from Magisterial documents regarding subdivisions within the diocesan territory[49], new expressions have been added to those of Parish and Vicariates Forane, which are foreseen in the current Code of Canon Law[50], namely "pastoral units" and "pastoral regions". These appellations effectively define new forms of pastoral organisation within a Diocese, thus reflecting a new relationship between the faithful and the territory.

44. In using terms like "pastoral units" and "pastoral regions", naturally one does not envisage that by simply giving a new name to already existing realities, a myriad of current problems are overcome. At the heart of a process of renewal, instead of passively undergoing change by supporting and going along with it, there exists today the need to individuate new structures that will incite all those who make up the Christian community to fulfil their vocation to evangelise, with a view to a more effective pastoral care of the People of God, the "key factor" of which is proximity.

---

[49] Cf. C.I.C., can. 374, §1.

[50] Cf. ibid., can. 374, §2; cf. also Congregation for Bishops, Directory for the Pastoral Ministry of Bishops *Apostolorum successores* (22nd February 2004), n. 217: *Enchiridion Vaticanum* 22 (2003-2004), 2110.

45. With this in mind, the canonical norm underlines the need to individuate different territories[51] within each Diocese, with the possibility of these being assembled into intermediate realities between a given Diocese and an individual Parish. Furthermore, by taking the size of the Diocese and its pastoral reality into account, one is better situated to delineate various kinds of Parish groupings[52].

The communal dimension of the Church lives and works at the heart of these groupings, with particular attention given to specific territories, the establishment of which must take into consideration the homogeneity and customs of the inhabitants, together with the common traits of the area, in order to foster a close relationship between Parish Priests and other pastoral workers[53].

VII. A. HOW TO PROCEED WITH THE ESTABLISHMENT OF PARISH GROUPINGS

46. Prior to establishing Parish groupings, the Bishop must first consult with the Presbyteral Council[54], in accord with canonical norms and in the name of ecclesial co-responsibility, shared between the Bishop and the members of said Council.

47. Firstly, the grouping together of various Parishes can take a simple federated form, whereby assembled Parishes would retain their own identity.

In accordance with canonical regulations, when one is grouping together neighbouring Parishes, naturally, the essential elements established by the universal law regarding the Parish as a juridical person must be observed and from which the Bishop cannot dispense[55]. For every Parish that the Bishop plans to

---

[51] Cf. C.I.C., can. 374, §1.

[52] Cf. ibid., can. 374, §2.

[53] Cf. *Apostolorum successores*, n. 218: *Enchiridion Vaticanum* 22 (2003-2004), 2114.

[54] Cf. C.I.C., can. 515, §2.

[55] Cf. ibid., can. 86.

supress, he must issue a specific decree to this effect, carefully outlining therein the motivating factors[56].

48. In light of the above, the grouping of Parishes, including their erection or suppression, is enacted by the diocesan Bishop, as envisioned by the norms of Canon Law, namely through extinctive union, where one Parish merges into another, being absorbed into it and losing its former individuality and juridical personality; alternatively, this can be effected through a true and proper fusion, that gives life to a new and unique Parish, resulting in the suppression of the existing Parishes and their juridical personality; or, finally, by division of a Parish community into several autonomous Parishes that are created *ex novo*[57].

Moreover, the suppression of Parishes by extinctive union is legitimate for causes directly related to a specific Parish. Some causes are not sufficient, such as, for example, the scarcity of diocesan clergy, the general financial situation of a Diocese, or other conditions within the community that are presumably reversible and of brief duration (e.g., numerical consistency, lack of financial self-sufficiency, the urban planning of the territory). As a condition for the legitimacy of this type of provision, the requisite motivations must be directly and organically connected to the interested Parish community, and not on general considerations or theories, or based solely "on principle".

49. Apropos of the erection or suppression of Parishes, it must be borne in mind that every decision must be adopted by means of a formal decree, given in writing[58]. Consequently, it is considered contrary to canonical norms to issue a single provision aimed at producing a reorganisation of a general character, either of the entire Diocese, a part of it, or of a group of Parishes, by means of a singular administrative act, general decree or particular law.

---

[56] Cf. ibid., can. 120, §1.

[57] Cf. ibid., cann. 121-122; cf. also *Apostolorum successores*, n. 214: *Enchiridion Vaticanum* 22 (2003-2004), 2099.

[58] Cf. C.I.C., can. 51.

50. With respect to the suppression of Parishes, the decree must clearly state the reasons that led the Bishop to make this decision. The just cause therefore, must be specifically indicated, it being insufficient simply to refer to the "good of souls".

The act by which a Parish is suppressed must also make provision for the disposition of temporal goods in accord with the law[59]; it is necessary to ensure that the Church of the suppressed Parish remains open to the faithful unless there are grave reasons to the contrary, after having heard the Presbyteral Council[60].

51. Related to the topic of Parish groupings and their possible suppression, is the necessity that sometimes occurs, of the reduction of Churches to profane but not sordid use[61], which belongs to the diocesan Bishop, after having first heard from the Presbyteral Council, whom he is obliged to consult[62].

Ordinarily, also in this case, the legitimate causes for decreeing such a reduction do not include reasons like the lack of clergy, demographic decline or the grave financial state of the Diocese. However, if the building is in such a state as to be unable to be used for divine worship in any way, and there is no possibility of repairing it, then the Bishop can proceed, according to the norm of law, to reduce it to profane but not sordid use.

VII. B. VICARIATE FORANE

52. It is necessary to recall here that "to foster pastoral care by means of common action, several neighbouring parishes can be joined together in special groups, such as vicariates forane"[63];

---

[59] Cf. ibid., cann. 120-123.

[60] Cf. ibid., cann. 500, §2 and 1222, §2.

[61] Cf. Pontifical Council for Culture, *Decommissioning and Ecclesial Reuse of Churches: Guidelines* (17th December 2018): *http://www.cultura.va/content/cultura/it/pub/documenti/decommissioning.html*

[62] Cf. C.I.C., can. 1222, §2.

[63] Ibid., can. 374, §2.

these are identified under various headings such as "deaneries", "pastoral zones" or "prefectures"[64].

53. The Vicar Forane does not necessarily have to be a Parish Priest of a specific Parish[65]. Furthermore, in order to achieve the purpose for which the vicariate is established, his primary responsibility is "to promote and coordinate common pastoral action in the vicariate"[66], so that it does not remain a purely formal institution. In addition, the Vicar Forane "is obliged to visit the Parishes of his district in accordance with the arrangement made by the diocesan Bishop"[67]. In order that he may better fulfil his function and promote common activity among Parishes, the diocesan Bishop may confer upon the Vicar Forane other faculties considered appropriate according to the specific circumstances.

VII. C. PASTORAL UNITS

54. Likewise, when circumstances require it, because of the expansive territory of the vicariate forane, or an increase in the number of the faithful, the Bishop, after hearing the Presbyteral Council[68], can decree a more stable and institutional grouping of various Parishes within the vicariate forane[69] in order to foster greater collaboration among them, bearing in mind the requisite criteria.

55. It is favourable that groupings (known as "pastoral units"[70]) are marked out in the best homogenous way possible, even from

---

[64] Cf. *Apostolorum successores*, n. 217: *Enchiridion Vaticanum* 22 (2003-2004), 2110.

[65] Cf. C.I.C., can. 554, §1.

[66] Ibid., can. 555, §1, 1°.

[67] Ibid., can. 555, §4.

[68] Cf. ibid., can. 500, §2.

[69] Cf. Pontifical Council for the Pastoral Care of Migrants and Itinerant People, *Erga migrantes caritas Christi* (3rd May 2004), n. 95; *Enchiridion Vaticanum* 22 (2003-2004), 2548.

[70] Cf. *Apostolorum successores*, n. 215: *Enchiridion Vaticanum* 22 (2003-2004), 2104.

a sociological point of view, in order to favour a more unified and cohesive[71] pastoral action that is missionary in nature.

56. Moreover, each Parish within such a grouping must be entrusted to a Parish Priest or to a group of priests *in solidum*, who would take care of the whole Parish community[72]. Alternatively, when deemed opportune by the Bishop, the grouping could be composed of several Parishes, each having the same Parish Priest[73].

57. In any case, due consideration must be given to priests who have exercised their ministry with merit and the esteem of their communities, also for the good of the faithful, bound as they are to their Pastors by ties of affection and gratitude. The diocesan Bishop, when establishing a particular grouping, must not establish in the same decree that, since several Parishes are being entrusted to a sole Parish Priest[74], that other Parish Priests, who may be present and still in office[75], are automatically transferred to the office of Parochial Vicar, or are removed de facto from their assignment.

58. In these cases, unless it concerns appointment *in solidum*, it belongs to the diocesan Bishop to define, on a case-by-case basis, the functions of the priest who is the leader of such parish groupings, as well as his collaboration with the Vicar Forane[76], thereby establishing the pastoral unit.

59. Once the grouping of Parishes has been established according to the norm of law – as either a vicariate forane or a "pastoral unit" – the Bishop will determine, as appropriate, whether each

---

[71] Cf. ibid.

[72] Cf. C.I.C., can. 517, §1.

[73] Cf. ibid., can. 526, §1.

[74] Cf. Ibid.

[75] Cf. Ibid., can. 522.

[76] Cf. ibid., cann. 553-555.

Parish should have its own Parish Pastoral Council[77], or whether it is better that this task be entrusted to a single Pastoral Council for all of them. In any case, the individual Parishes within the grouping, since they retain juridical personality and capacity, must maintain their own Finance Councils[78].

60. In order to prioritise evangelisation and a more effective pastoral care, it is appropriate that common pastoral services be established in certain areas (for example, catechesis, charity, youth or family pastoral care) for those Parishes within the grouping; with the participation of all the components of the People of God, namely clergy, consecrated men and women and the lay faithful.

VII. D. PASTORAL REGIONS

61. If several "pastoral units" can constitute a vicariate forane, then similarly, especially in Dioceses with a more extensive territory, the Bishop, after hearing the Presbyteral Council[79], could unite several vicariates forane into "districts" or "pastoral regions"[80]. An Episcopal Vicar[81] would lead each region, invested with ordinary executive power for pastoral administration in the Bishop's name, under his authority and in communion with him, and with any special faculties that the Bishop may wish to attribute to him.

---

[77] Cf. ibid., can. 536.

[78] Cf. ibid., can. 537.

[79] Cf. ibid., can. 500, §2.

[80] Cf. *Apostolorum successores*, n. 219: *Enchiridion Vaticanum* 22 (2003-2004), 2117; it is convenient to reserve the title of "pastoral region" for this kind of grouping alone, thus avoiding unnecessary confusion.

[81] Cf. C.I.C., cann. 134, §1 and 476.

VIII. ORDINARY AND EXTRAORDINARY WAYS OF ASSIGNING THE PASTORAL CARE OF THE PARISH COMMUNITY

62. In the first place, the Parish Priest and the other priests, in communion with the Bishop, are a fundamental reference point for the Parish community, for the role of shepherds that corresponds to them[82]. The Parish Priest and the presbyterate, who together foster a common life and priestly fraternity, celebrate the sacramental life for and with the community, and are called to organise the Parish in such a way as to be an effective sign of communion[83].

63. Regarding the presence and mission of priests in the Parish community, the common life deserves special mention[84]; it is recommended by can. 280, even if this is not an obligation for the secular clergy. In this respect, it is worth recalling the fundamental value of the spirit of communion, prayer and common pastoral activity on the part of clerics[85], with a view to an effective witness of sacramental brotherhood[86] and a more effective evangelising action.

---

[82] It should be noted that: a) what is said in reference to the "diocesan Bishop" is valid also for all those equal to him in law; b) what is said about the Parish or the Parish Priest is also valid for quasi-Parishes and quasi-Parish Priests; c) what concerns the lay faithful applies also to members of non-clerical institutes of consecrated life or societies of apostolic life, unless specific reference is being made to the secular; d) the term "Moderator" has different meanings based on the context in which it is used in this present Instruction, in accord with the norms of the code.

[83] Cf. *Lumen gentium*, n. 26: AAS 57 (1965), 31-32.

[84] Cf. *Ratio fundamentalis institutionis sacerdotalis*, ns. 83; 88.e, pp. 37; 39.

[85] Cf. C.I.C., can. 275, §1.

[86] Cf. Second Vatican Ecumenical Council, Decree on the ministry and life of priests *Presbyterorum ordinis* (7th December 1965), n. 8: AAS 58 (1966), 1003.

64. When the presbyterate experiences community life, priestly identity is strengthened, material concerns diminish, and the temptation of individualism gives way to profoundly personal relationships. Common prayer, shared reflection and study, which must never be lacking in priestly life, can be of great support in the formation of an incarnate priestly spirituality in daily living.

In any case, it will be fitting that, according to his discernment and as far as possible, the Bishop take into account the human and spiritual affinity between priests to whom he intends to entrust a Parish or a grouping of Parishes, inviting them to a generous availability for their new pastoral mission in a common brotherhood[87].

65. In some cases, especially where the tradition or the custom of a presbytery is lacking, or when for some reason such a dwelling is unavailable, it may happen that a priest returns to live with his family of origin, that first place of human formation and vocational discovery[88].

On the one hand, this arrangement can have a positive effect on the priest's daily life, in that he is assured of a serene and stable home environment, especially when his parents are still living. On the other hand, the priest must ensure that he does not become dependent on these familial relationships, which could negatively affect his availability for full-time mission, his relationship with the presbyteral family and the community of the lay faithful.

---

[87] Cf. *Ratio fundamentalis institutionis sacerdotalis*, n. 88, pp. 39-40.

[88] Cf. Francis, Address to participants in the Convention sponsored by the Congregation for the Clergy on the 50th anniversary of the Conciliar Decrees *"Optatam totius"* and *"Presbyterorum ordinis"* (20th November 2015): AAS 107 (2015), 1295.

VIII. A. PARISH PRIEST

66. The office of Parish Priest, sometimes referred to as Pastor, involves the full care of souls[89]. In order, therefore, for a member of the faithful to be validly appointed Parish Priest (*parochus*), he must have received the Order of Presbyter[90], thus excluding the possibility of conferring this office on one who lacks this Order and its related functions, even where priests are scarce.

Precisely because of the relationship of familiarity and closeness that is required between a pastor and the community, the office of Parish Priest cannot be entrusted to a juridical person[91]. Apart from what is envisioned by can. 517, §§1-2, the particular office of Parish Priest may not be entrusted to a group composed of clerics and lay people. Consequently, appellations such as "team leader", "équipe leader", or the like, which convey a sense of collegial government of the Parish, are to be avoided.

67. As a consequence of his being the "pastor of the Parish entrusted to him"[92], the Parish Priest is *ipso iure* the legal representative of the Parish[93]. He is the administrator responsible for the parish goods, which are "ecclesiastical goods", therefore subject to the relevant canonical norms[94].

68. As the Second Vatican Ecumenical Council affirmed, "Pastors should enjoy in their respective parishes that stability of office which the good of souls demands"[95]. As a general principle, the Parish Priest ought to be "appointed for an indeterminate period of time"[96].

---

[89] Cf. C.I.C., can. 150.

[90] Cf. ibid., can. 521, §1.

[91] Cf. ibid., can. 520, §1.

[92] Ibid., can. 519.

[93] Cf. ibid., can. 532.

[94] Cf. ibid., can. 1257, §1.

[95] *Christus Dominus*, n. 31: AAS 58 (1965), 689.

[96] C.I.C., can. 522.

The diocesan Bishop, however, can appoint Parish Priests for a determined period, if this has been established by decree of the Episcopal Conference. Because of the need for the Parish Priest to be able to establish an effective bond with the community entrusted to him, it is fitting that Episcopal Conferences not establish too short a period, preferably no less than five years for a fixed-term appointment.

69. In any case, Parish Priests, even if appointed indefinitely, or before the expiry of his fixed term, must be available for a possible transfer to another Parish or office, if "the good of souls or the necessity or advantage of the Church demands"[97]. It should be recalled that the Parish Priest is at the service of the Parish, and not the other way around.

70. Ordinarily, it is good that the Parish Priest, where possible, have the pastoral care of only one Parish, "however, because of a shortage of priests or other circumstances, the care of a number of neighbouring Parishes can be entrusted to a single Parish Priest"[98]. For example, "other circumstances" may include the small size of the territory or population, as well as proximity to neighbouring Parishes. The diocesan Bishop should carefully evaluate whether the Parish Priest who is entrusted with the care of several Parishes can fully and truly exercise the office of Parish Priest for each and for all of them[99].

71. Once appointed, the Parish Priest remains in the full exercise of the functions entrusted to him, with all the rights and responsibilities thereof, until he has legitimately ceased his pastoral office[100]. For his removal, or transfer, before the expiry of his mandate, the relevant canonical procedures must

---

[97] Ibid., can. 1748.

[98] Ibid., can. 526, §1.

[99] Cf. ibid., can. 152.

[100] Cf. ibid., can. 538, §§1-2.

be observed, which serve the Church as a discernment of what is appropriate in specific cases[101].

72. When the good of the faithful requires it, even if there are no other causes for cessation, the Parish Priest who has reached seventy-five years of age should accept the invitation from the diocesan Bishop to resign from the Parish[102]. The presentation of the renunciation, upon having reached seventy-five years of age[103], is to be considered a moral duty, if not canonical, although it does not mean the Parish Priest ceases from his office automatically. The cessation of office occurs only when the diocesan Bishop has informed the said Parish Priest, in writing, of the acceptance of his resignation[104]. For his part, the Bishop should kindly consider the resignation presented by a Parish Priest, if for no other reason than he has reached seventy-five years of age.

73. In order then, to avoid a conception of ministry that is purely functional, the diocesan Bishop, prior to accepting the renunciation, will prudently weigh up all the circumstances of person and place, like those of health or disciplinary reasons, the shortage of priests, the good of the Parish community and other such elements, subsequently accepting the resignation for a just and proportionate cause[105].

74. If the personal condition of the priest permits and if it is pastorally feasible, the Bishop could consider the possibility of leaving him in the office of Parish Priest, perhaps with some assistance that would eventually pave the way for his succession. Furthermore, "depending on the circumstances, the Bishop may entrust a smaller and less demanding parish to a

---

[101] Cf. ibid., cann. 1740-1752, keeping in mind cann. 190-195.

[102] Cf. ibid., can. 538, §3.

[103] Ibid.

[104] Cf. ibid., can. 189.

[105] Cf. ibid., can. 189, §2 and *Apostolorum successores*, n. 212: *Enchiridion Vaticanum* 22 (2003-2004), 2095.

pastor who has resigned"[106], or in any case assign him another pastoral task appropriate to his circumstances, helping him, if need be, to understand that in no way should he feel "demoted" or "punished" by a transfer of this kind.

VIII. B. PARISH ADMINISTRATOR

75. If it is not possible to proceed immediately with the appointment of the Parish Priest, the appointment of Parish Administrators[107] must be done only in conformity with what is established in the canonical norms[108].

In effect, the office is essentially transitory and is exercised while awaiting the appointment of the new Parish Priest. For this reason, it is illegitimate for the diocesan Bishop to appoint a Parish Administrator and to leave him in that position for an extended period of time, more than a year, or even permanently, in order to avoid the appointment of a Parish Priest.

As experience shows, this solution is often adopted in order to circumvent the requirements of the law regarding the principle of stability for the Parish Priest, which constitutes a violation, with harm to both the mission of the priest and that of the community itself. Because of the uncertainty about the presence of a pastor, the Parish is not able to programme far-reaching evangelisation plans and must limit its pastoral care to mere preservation.

VIII. C. PRIESTS IN SOLIDUM

76. As a further possibility, "where circumstances so require, the pastoral care of a parish, or of a number of parishes together, can be entrusted to several priests jointly"[109]. Such a solution can be

---

[106] *Apostolorum successores*, n. 212: *Enchiridion Vaticanum* 22 (2003-2004), 2095.

[107] Cf. C.I.C., cann. 539-540.

[108] Cf. in particular ibid., cann. 539, 549, 1747, §3.

[109] Ibid., can. 517, §1; cf. also cann. 542-544.

adopted when, at the Bishop's discretion, concrete circumstances require it so, particularly for the good of the communities concerned, through shared and more effective pastoral action, and to promote a spirituality of communion among priests[110].

In such cases, the group of priests, in communion with the other members of the Parish community, act in common deliberation, the Moderator being a *primus inter pares* among the other priests, all of whom are, to all intents and purposes, Parish Priests.

77. It is strongly recommended that each community of priests, to whom the pastoral care of one or more Parishes is entrusted *in solidum*, should draw up internal rules so that each priest can better carry out the tasks and functions to which he is assigned[111].

The Moderator is responsible for coordinating the joint work of the Parish or Parishes entrusted to the group. Moreover, as their juridical representative[112], he is to coordinate the exercise of the faculty to assist at marriages, grant dispensations, as would Parish Priests[113], and give a report to the Bishop on all the activities of the group[114].

VIII. D. PAROCHIAL VICAR

78. Additionally, a priest may be appointed as a Parochial Vicar (also called an Assistant Priest, a Curate, an Associate Pastor, etc.) with responsibility for a sector of pastoral care (the youth, the elderly, the sick, associations, confraternities, formation, catechesis, etc.) across different parishes, or to assist with the entire ministry, or only part of it, in one parish;[115].

---

[110] Cf. ibid., cann. 517, §1 and 526, §1.

[111] Cf. ibid., can. 543, §1.

[112] Cf., ibid., can. 543, §2, 3°; In countries where the Parish is recognised by the State as a juridical entity, he would also assume the role of the civil juridical representative.

[113] Cf., ibid., can. 543, §1.

[114] Cf. ibid., can. 517, §1.

[115] Cf. ibid., can. 545, §2; one can think here of a priest who is experienced in the field of spirituality, who, due to poor health, could be appointed as an ordinary Confessor to five adjoining territorial Parishes.

With regard to a Parochial Vicar being assigned to several Parishes, which have different Parish Priests, it will be necessary to explain and describe, in the decree of appointment, the tasks entrusted to him in relation to each Parish community, as well as the type of collaboration to be had with each Parish Priest in terms of his residence, sustenance and the celebration of Holy Mass.

VIII. E. DEACONS

79. Deacons are ordained ministers, incardinated in a Diocese, or in some other ecclesial reality that has the faculty to do so[116]. They are collaborators of the Bishop and the priests in a singular mission of evangelisation and with the specific task, by virtue of the Sacrament received, to "serve the People of God in the ministries of the liturgy, the word and charity"[117].

80. In order to safeguard the identity of deacons, with a view to promoting their ministry, Pope Francis highlighted several risks related to how the nature of the diaconate is understood: "But we must be careful not to see deacons as half-priests, half-laymen. [...] Likewise, the image of the deacon as a sort of intermediary between the faithful and pastors is inappropriate. Neither halfway between priests and laypeople, nor halfway between pastors and faithful. There is the danger of clericalism: the deacon who is too clerical [...] And another temptation is functionalism: it is a help that the priest has for this or that"[118].

In that same address, the Holy Father offered some clarifications regarding the specific role of deacons within the ecclesial community: "The diaconate is a specific vocation, a family vocation that requires service [...] This word is the key to

---

[116] Cf. ibid., can. 265.

[117] Ibid., can. 1009, §3.

[118] Francis, Encounter with priests and consecrated persons, Milan (25th March 2017): AAS 109 (2017), 376.

understanding your charism. Service as one of the characteristic gifts of the people of God. The deacon is, so to say, the custodian of service in the Church. Every word must be carefully measured. You are the guardians of service in the Church: service to the Word, service to the altar, service to the poor"[119].

81. Teaching on the diaconate has evolved significantly over the centuries. Its resumption at the Second Vatican Council coincided with a doctrinal clarification and expansion, which no longer "limited" the diaconate to charitable service alone or defined it, as did the Council of Trent, as transitional and almost exclusively identified with liturgical service. The Second Vatican Council specified that it is a degree of the Sacrament of Holy Orders and that, consequently, deacons "strengthened by sacramental grace, in communion with the bishop and his group of priests [...], serve in the diaconate of the liturgy, of the word, and of charity to the people of God"[120].

The post-conciliar reception takes up what was established by *Lumen gentium*, further elucidating how the office of deacons is a participation in the Sacrament of Holy Orders, albeit to a different degree. In an audience with participants at the International Congress on the Diaconate, Paul VI reaffirmed that the deacon serves Christian communities "in proclaiming the Word of God, in sacramental ministry and in the exercise of charity"[121]. In turning to the Acts of the Apostles (6:1-6), it would appear that the seven chosen men are destined only for table service; in reality, the same biblical Book recounts how Stephen and Philip carried out the "diaconia of the Word" in their own right. Therefore, as collaborators of the Twelve and of Paul, they exercised their ministry in two areas: evangelisation and charity.

---

[119] Ibid., 376-377.

[120] *Lumen gentium*, n. 29: AAS 57 (1965), 36.

[121] Paul VI, Address to the participants of the International Congress on the Diaconate, 25th October 1965: *Enchiridion on the Diaconate* (2009), 147-148.

There are many ecclesial tasks, therefore, that can be entrusted to a deacon, namely, all those that do not involve the full care of souls[122]. The *Code of Canon Law*, however, determines which offices are reserved to the priest and those that can also be entrusted to the lay faithful, while there is no indication of any particular office in which the deacon's ministry can find specific expression.

82. In any case, the history of the diaconate recalls that it was established within the framework of a ministerial vision of the Church, as an ordained ministry at the service of the Word and of charity; this latter context includes the administration of goods. The twofold mission of the deacon is expressed in the liturgical sphere, where he is called to proclaim the Gospel and to serve at the Eucharistic table. These references can help identify the specific tasks of a deacon, adding value to that which is proper to the diaconate, with a view to promoting the diaconal ministry.

VIII. F. CONSECRATED MEN AND WOMEN

83. Oftentimes, within the Parish community, there are persons belonging to the consecrated life. "This is not a reality external to or independent of the life of the local Church; rather it constitutes a particular way of being in the midst of the local Church, which is marked by the radicalness of the Gospel and which possesses its own specific gifts"[123]. Moreover, integrated into the community with clerics and laity, consecrated life "is located within the charismatic dimension of the Church [...] The spirituality of the Institutes of Consecrated Life can become for both the lay faithful and the priest a significant resource enabling them to live their own proper vocation"[124].

---

[122] Cf. C.I.C., can. 150.

[123] Congregation for the Doctrine of the Faith, Letter *Iuvenescit ecclesia* to the Bishops of the Catholic Church regarding the relationship between hierarchical and charismatic gifts in the life and the mission of the Church (15th May 2016), n. 21: *Enchiridion Vaticanum* 32 (2016), 734.

[124] Ibid., n. 22: *Enchiridion Vaticanum* 32 (2016), 738.

84. The contribution that consecrated men and women can bring to the evangelising mission of the Parish community is derived firstly, from their "being", that is, from the witness of a radical following of Christ through the profession of the evangelical counsels[125], and only secondly from their "doing", that is, from the works carried out in accordance with the charism of each Institute (for example, catechesis, charity, formation, youth ministry, care of the sick)[126].

VIII. G. THE LAITY

85. The Parish community is composed in a particular way of the lay faithful[127], who, by virtue of their Baptism and the other Sacraments of Christian initiation, and in many cases by matrimony[128], participate in the evangelising action of the Church, since "the essential vocation and mission of the lay faithful is to strive that earthly realities and all human activity may be transformed by the Gospel"[129].

In a particular way, the lay faithful, who have a specific secular character, "seek the Kingdom of God by engaging in temporal affairs and by ordering them according to the plan of God"[130]. They "can also feel themselves called, or be called, to work with their pastors in the service of the ecclesial community for its growth and life, by exercising a great variety of ministries according to the grace and charisms which the Lord is pleased to give them"[131].

---

[125] Cf. C.I.C., can. 573, §1.

[126] Cf. Congregation for Institutes of Consecrated Life and Societies of Apostolic Life – Congregation for Bishops, *Mutuae relationes*. Directives for the mutual relations between Bishops and Religious in the Church (14th May 1978), ns. 10; 14, a): *Enchiridion Vaticanum* 6 (1977-1979), 604-605; 617-620; cf. also *Apostolorum successores*, n. 98: *Enchiridion Vaticanum* 22 (2003-2004), 1803-1804.

[127] Cf. *Evangelii gaudium*, n. 102: AAS 105 (2013), 1062-1063.

[128] Cf. *Christifideles laici*, n. 23: AAS 81 (1989), 429.

[129] *Evangelii gaudium*, n. 201: AAS 105 (2013), 1104.

[130] *Lumen gentium*, n. 31: AAS 57 (1965), 37.

[131] Paul VI, Apostolic Exortation *Evangelii nuntiandi* (8th December 1975), n. 73: AAS 68 (1976), 61.

86. The lay faithful are called upon in our present age to make a generous commitment to the service of the mission of evangelisation, first of all through the general witness of their daily lives, lived in conformity with the Gospel, in whatever environment they are in and at every level of responsibility; in a particular way, they are called to place themselves at the service of the Parish community[132].

VIII. H. OTHER FORMS OF ASSIGNING PASTORAL CARE

87. There is a further way for the Bishop to provide for the pastoral care of a community, as can be seen from can. 517 §, 2, when it is not possible to appoint a full-time Parish Priest or a Parish Administrator, due to a shortage of priests. In such pastorally problematic circumstances, in order to sustain Christian life and to continue the evangelising mission of the community, the diocesan Bishop may entrust the pastoral care of a Parish to a deacon, to a consecrated religious or layperson, or even to a group of persons (e.g., Religious Institute, Association)[133].

88. Those entrusted with participation in the exercise of the pastoral care of the community will be directed by a priest with legitimate faculties, who will act as a "Moderator of Pastoral Care", with the powers and functions of a Parish Priest, albeit without an office with its duties and rights.

It should be remembered that we are dealing here with an extraordinary form of entrusting pastoral care, due to the impossibility of appointing a Parish Priest or a Parish Administrator, which is not to be confused with the ordinary active cooperation of the lay faithful in assuming their responsibilities.

89. In view of this extraordinary remedy, the People of God should be adequately prepared in this regard, cognisant that

---

[132] Cf. *Evangelii gaudium*, n. 81: AAS 105 (2013), 1053-1054.

[133] Cf. C.I.C., can. 517, §2.

it is a temporary and not a permanent measure[134]. The correct understanding and application of this canon requires that this exceptional provision "be used only with strict adherence to conditions contained in it. These are: a) *ob sacerdotum penuriam* and not for reasons of convenience or ambiguous 'advancement of the laity' [...]; b) this is *participatio in exercitio curae pastoralis* and not directing, coordinating, moderating or governing the Parish; these competencies, according to the canon, are the competencies of a priest alone"[135].

90. In order to ensure a successful outcome in the assignment of pastoral care according to canon 517 §2[136], certain criteria must be observed. Since this is an extraordinary and temporary pastoral solution[137], the only canonical cause that makes recourse to it legitimate is a lack of priests to provide pastoral care for the Parish community in the appointment of a Parish Priest or Parish Administrator. Furthermore, it would be preferable to appoint one or more deacons over consecrated men and women or laypersons for directing this kind of pastoral care[138].

91. At any rate, the coordination of pastoral activity organised in this way falls to the priest who is appointed as the Moderator

---

[134] Cf. *Apostolorum successores*, n. 215, c): *Enchiridion Vaticanum* 22 (2003-2004), 2105.

[135] Congregation for the Clergy, Instruction [Interdicasterial] on certain questions regarding the collaboration of the non-ordained faithful in the sacred ministry of priest *Ecclesiae de mysterio* (15th August 1997), art. 4, §1, a-b): AAS 89 (1997), 866-867; cf. also *Apostolorum successores*, n. 215, c): *Enchiridion Vaticanum* 22 (2003-2004), 2105. The priest will also have the legal representation of the Parish, both canonically and civilly, when foreseen by the Law of the State.

[136] Before resorting to the provision of can. 517, §2, the diocesan Bishop should prudently consider other alternative possibilities, like availing of senior priests who are still valid for ministry, or entrusting several Parishes to a single Parish Priest or several Parishes to a group of priests *in solidum*.

[137] Cf. *Ecclesiae de mysterio*, art. 4, § 1, b): AAS 89 (1997), 866-867, and Congregation for the Clergy, Instruction *The Priest, Pastor and Leader of the Parish Community* (4th August 2002), ns. 23 and 25, regarding "collaboration *ad tempus* in the exercise of the pastoral care of a parish", cf. n. 23: *Enchiridion Vaticanum* 21 (2002), 834-836.

[138] Cf. *The Priest, Pastor and Leader of the Parish Community*, n. 25: *Enchiridion Vaticanum* 21 (2002), 836.

by the diocesan Bishop; this priest alone has the powers and faculties proper to the Parish Priest; the other members of the faithful, on the other hand, have "a share in the exercise of the pastoral care of a Parish"[139].

92. The deacon, together with those who have not received Holy Orders and who participate in the exercise of pastoral care, are to perform only those functions which correspond to their respective status as deacons or lay faithful, ensuring that "the original properties of diversity and complementarity of the charisms and functions of ordained ministers and the lay faithful must be carefully observed and respected since these are proper to the Church and are willed by God for its organisation"[140].

93. Finally, in the decree by which he appoints the Moderator Priest, it is strongly recommended that the Bishop would set out, at least briefly, the reasons why it has become necessary to apply this extraordinary form to the assignment of pastoral care to one or more Parish communities, together with the kinds of ministry that the priest in charge will exercise.

---

[139] C.I.C., can. 517, §2.

[140] *The Priest, Pastor and Leader of the Parish Community*, n. 23: *Enchiridion Vaticanum* 21 (2002), 834.

IX. APPOINTMENTS AND PASTORAL MINISTRY

94. Besides the occasional collaboration that every person of good will — even the unbaptised — may offer in the daily activities of the Parish, there exist also stable appointments, on the basis of which the faithful accept responsibility for service within the Parish community for a determined time. For example, one thinks of catechists, of altar servers, of educators that work in groups and associations, of those who fulfil the works of charity and those who dedicate themselves to different types of counselling or to listening centres, and of those who visit the sick.

95. In any case, in designating the tasks entrusted to deacons, consecrated men and women and the lay faithful that receive a participation in the exercise of pastoral care, it is necessary to use terminology that corresponds in a correct way to the functions that they can fulfil in conformity with their state of life. In this way, the essential difference that exists between the common priesthood and the ministerial priesthood is clearly maintained, and the identity of the appointment received by each person should be evident.

96. In that vein, it is the responsibility, first of all, of the diocesan Bishop and, as far as it pertains to him, the Parish Priest, to see that the appointments of deacons, religious and laity that have roles of responsibility in the Parish, are not designated as "pastor", "co-pastor", "chaplain", "moderator", "coordinator", "Parish manager", or other similar terms[141] reserved by law to priests,[142] inasmuch as they have a direct correlation to the ministerial profile of priests.

---

[141] Cf. *Ecclesia de mysterio*, art. 1 §3: AAS 89 (1997), 863.

[142] Cf. *The Priest, Pastor and Leader of the Parish Community*, n. 23: *Enchiridion Vaticanum* 21 (2002), 835.

In referring to the aforementioned faithful and deacons, it is likewise illegitimate, and not in conformity with their vocational identity, to use expressions such as "entrust the pastoral care of a parish", "preside over the parish community", and other similar phrases, that pertain to the distinct sacerdotal ministry of a Parish Priest.

For example, the terms "Deacon Cooperator" or "Coordinator of (a particular sector of pastoral care)", "Pastoral Cooperator" or "Pastoral Associate or Assistant" seem to be more appropriate.

97. Lay men, by the norms of law, may be instituted Lectors or Acolytes on a stable basis, by means of the relevant rite, according to canon 230 §1. The non-ordained faithful may use the term "extraordinary minister" only if called by the competent Authority[143] to fulfil the supplementary functions referred to in canons 230 §3 and 943. The temporary deputation in liturgical celebrations, which canon 230 §2 mentions, even if protracted for some time, does not confer any special designation on the non-ordained faithful[144].

These laypersons must be in full communion with the Catholic Church[145], receive a formation adequate to the function that they are called to perform, and maintain a personal and pastoral conduct that is exemplary, making them convincing in carrying out their service.

98. In addition to what pertains to stably instituted Lectors and Acolytes[146], the Bishop, according to his prudent judgement, may

---

[143] Cf. *Apostolorum successores*, n. 112: *Enchiridion Vaticanum* 22 (2003-2004), 1843.

[144] It is worth remembering that, in addition to the ministry of Lector for men, among the liturgical functions which the diocesan Bishop, after consulting the Episcopal Conference, can temporarily entrust to the lay faithful (men and women), there is also the service at the altar, in accordance with the relevant canonical norm; cf. Pontifical Council for Legislative Texts, Response (11th July 1992): AAS 86 (1994), 541; Congregation for Divine Worship and the Discipline of the Sacraments, Circular Letter (15th March 1994): AAS 86 (1994), 541-542.

[145] Cf. C.I.C. can. 205.

[146] Cf. ibid., can. 230 §1.

officially entrust to deacons, consecrated men and women and lay faithful, under the direction and responsibility of the Parish Priest, other duties[147] such as:

1. The celebration of the Liturgy of the Word on Sundays and Holy Days of Obligation, when "participation in the Eucharistic celebration becomes impossible because of the absence of a sacred minister or for another grave cause"[148]. This is considered an exceptional eventuality, recourse to which is made only in circumstances of true impossibility and always taking care to entrust these liturgies to deacons, if they are present;

2. The administration of Baptism, with due consideration for the fact that, "the ordinary minister of baptism is a bishop, priest or deacon"[149] and that what is provided in canon 861 §2 constitutes an exception, to be evaluated at the discretion of the local Ordinary;

3. The celebration of funeral rites, as provided in n.19 of the Praenotanda of the *Order of Christian Funerals*.

99. The lay faithful may preach in a Church or oratory, if circumstances, necessity or a particular case call for it, "according to the prescripts of the Episcopal Conference"[150] and "when expressly permitted by law or liturgical norms, as long as conditions contained in them are observed"[151]. However, these individuals may not in any case give the homily during the celebration of the Eucharist[152].

---

[147] In the act by which the Bishop entrusts the tasks mentioned above to deacons or lay faithful, he is to determine clearly the functions they are enabled to fulfil and for how long.

[148] C.I.C. can. 1248 §2.

[149] Ibid., can. 861 §1.

[150] Ibid., can. 766.

[151] *Ecclesia de mysterio*, art. 3 §4: AAS 89 (1997), 865.

[152] Cf. C.I.C. can. 767 §1; cf. also *Ecclesia de mysterio*, art. 3 §1: AAS 89 (1997), 864.

100. Moreover, "where there is a lack of priests and deacons, the diocesan Bishop can delegate lay persons to assist at marriages, with the previous favourable vote of the Episcopal Conference and after obtaining the permission of the Holy See"[153].

---

[153] C.I.C. can. 1112 §1; cf. John Paul II, Apostolic Constitution *Pastor bonus* (28th June 1998), art. 63: AAS 80 (1988), 876, regarding the competence of the Congregation for Divine Worship and the Discipline of the Sacraments.

X. BODIES OF ECCLESIAL CO-RESPONSIBILITY

X. A. THE PARISH FINANCE COUNCIL

101. The administration of goods which every Parish has to some extent is an important area of evangelisation and evangelical witness, both in the Church and in civil society, since "all the goods that we have, the Lord gives them to go to the world, to go to humanity, to help others"[154]. The Parish Priest, therefore, cannot and must not remain only at this task[155], so it is necessary that he be assisted by collaborators to administer the goods of the Church above all with evangelising zeal and a missionary spirit.[156]

102. For this reason, in every Parish a Finance Council must be constituted as a consultative body, presided over by the Parish Priest and formed of at least three other faithful[157]; the minimum number of three is necessary so that this Council may be considered "collegial". It bears recalling that the Parish Priest is not counted among the members of the Finance Council, but he presides over it.

103. Absent specific norms issued by the diocesan Bishop, it will be for the Parish Priest to determine the number of members of this Council, relative to the size of the Parish, and whether these should be appointed by him, or elected somehow by the Parish community.

---

[154] Francis, Daily Meditation at the Casa Santa Marta (21st October 2013): *L'Osservatore Romano* 242 (21st-22nd October 2013), 8.

[155] Cf. C.I.C. cann. 537 and 1280.

[156] In conformity with C.I.C. canon 532, the Parish Priest is responsible for the goods of the Parish, even if in administering them, he must avail himself of the collaboration of lay experts.

[157] Cf. C.I.C. can. 115 §2 and, by analogy, can. 492 §1.

The members of this Council, not necessarily belonging to the Parish itself, must be of proven good reputation, and expert in financial and legal questions[158], so as to render an effective and competent service, in such a way that the Council is not established as a mere formality.

104. Unless the diocesan Bishop has decided otherwise, observing the necessary prudence and any pertinent norms of civil law, nothing prevents the same person from being a member of the Finance Council of multiple Parishes, whenever circumstances require.

105. Any eventual norms issued by the diocesan Bishop in these matters must take account of the specific situations of Parishes, such as, for example, those of particularly modest means, or those forming part of a pastoral unit[159].

106. The Finance Council fulfils a role of particular importance in the growth, at the level of the Parish community, of a culture of co-responsibility, of administrative transparency, and of service to the needs of the Church. In a particular way, transparency should not be understood as a mere formal presentation of statistics, but more as information that is the community's due, and an advantageous opportunity for its formative involvement. Transparency refers to a *modus agendi*, indispensable for the credibility of the Church, especially where there are significant goods to administer.

107. Ordinarily, the goal of transparency may be attained by publishing the annual financial report that must first be presented to the local Ordinary[160], with detailed indications of income and expenditure. From the annual report, the community as a whole may be aware that these goods belong to the Parish, not the Parish

---

[158] Cf. ibid., can. 537 and *Apostolorum successores*, n. 210: *Enchiridion Vaticanum* 22 (2003-2004), 2087.

[159] Cf. C.I.C. cann. 517 and 526.

[160] Cf. ibid., can. 1287 §1.

Priest; that he is the steward of them; how they are administered; what the financial situation of the Parish is and what resources are effectively at its disposal.

X. B. THE PARISH PASTORAL COUNCIL

108. The current canonical norms[161] leave it to the diocesan Bishop to decide on the establishment of a Pastoral Council in Parishes, but in any case, they may ordinarily be considered as highly recommended, as Pope Francis recalled, "How necessary pastoral councils are! A Bishop cannot guide a Diocese without pastoral councils. A Parish Priest cannot guide without pastoral councils"[162].

The flexibility of the norm permits the adaptation considered apt for the concrete circumstances, as for example, in the case of multiple Parishes entrusted to a single Parish Priest, or those within pastoral units: it is possible in this cases to establish a single Pastoral Council for several Parishes.

109. The theological significance of the Pastoral Council is inscribed in the constitutive reality of the Church, that is, in her being "the Body of Christ", that generates a "spirituality of communion". In the Christian community, in fact, the diversity of charisms and ministries that derive from incorporation into Christ and from the gift of the Holy Spirit may never be homogenised until they become "uniformity, the obligation of doing everything together and all as equals, of always thinking the same thing in the same way"[163]. On the contrary, in virtue of the baptismal priesthood[164], every member of the faithful is created for the building up of the whole Body and, at the same

---

[161] Cf. ibid., can. 536 §1.

[162] Francis, Discourse during the meeting with clergy, consecrated persons and members of pastoral councils, Assisi (4th October 2013): Insegnamenti I/2 (2013), 328.

[163] Id., Homily at the Mass of the Solemnity of Pentecost, 4th June 2017: AAS 109 (2017), 711.

[164] Cf. *Lumen gentium*, n. 10: AAS 57 (1965), 14.

time, the whole People of God, in the reciprocal co-responsibility of its members, participates in the mission of the Church, that is, discerning in history the signs of the presence of God and becoming witnesses of his Kingdom[165].

110. Far from being simply a bureaucratic organ, the Pastoral Council highlights and realizes the centrality of the People of God as the subject and active protagonist of the evangelising mission, in virtue of the fact that every member of the faithful has received the gifts of the Spirit through Baptism and Confirmation: "Rebirth to the divine life of baptism is the first step; next comes conducting ourselves as children of God, namely, by conforming ourselves to Christ who works in Holy Church, letting ourselves be involved in her mission in the world. To that end, the anointing of the Spirit is provided: 'without your strength, we have none' (cf. Pentecost Sequence). [...] As Jesus was animated by the Spirit for his whole life, so also the life of the Church and of each of her members is under the guidance of the same Spirit"[166].

In light of this fundamental vision, the words of Saint Paul VI come to mind, "It is the function of the pastoral council to investigate everything pertaining to pastoral activities, to weigh them carefully and to set forth practical conclusions concerning them so as to promote conformity of the life and actions of the People of God with the Gospel"[167], in the awareness that, as Pope Francis recalled, the purpose of such a Council "should not be ecclesiastical organisation but rather the missionary aspiration of reaching everyone"[168].

---

[165] Cf. Congregation for the Clergy, Circular Letter *Omnes Christifideles* (25th January 1973), ns. 4 and 9: *Enchiridion Vaticanum* 4 (1971-1973), 1199-1201 and 1207-1209; cf. also *Christifideles laici*, n. 27: AAS 81 (1989), 440-441.

[166] Francis, General Audience (23rd May 2018).

[167] Paul VI, Apostolic Letter Motu Proprio, *Ecclesiae sanctae* (6th August 1966), I, 16 §1: AAS 58 (1966), 766; cf. aslo C.I.C. can. 511.

[168] *Evangelii gaudium*, n. 31: AAS 105 (2013), 1033.

111. The Pastoral Council is a consultative body, governed by the norms established by the diocesan Bishop, to define the criteria of its composition, the methods of election of its members, its objectives and manner of functioning[169]. In any case, in order not to distort the nature of this Council, it is best to avoid defining it as a "team" or "équipe", that is to say in terms that are not suitable to express concretely the ecclesial and canonical relationship between the Parish Priest and the rest of the faithful.

112. With regard to the relative diocesan norms, it is necessary that the Pastoral Council effectively represent the community of which it is an expression in its membership (priests, deacons, religious and laity). This constitutes a specific setting in which the faithful are able to exercise their right and duty to express their own thought concerning the good of the Parish community to the pastors[170], and to communicate it to other members of the faithful.

113. The Parish Pastoral Council "possesses a consultative vote only"[171], in the sense that its proposals must be accepted favourably by the Parish Priest to become operative. The Parish Priest is then bound to consider the indications of the Pastoral Council attentively, especially if they express themselves unanimously, in a process of common discernment.

So that the service of the Pastoral Council might be efficacious and fruitful, it is necessary to avoid two extremes: on one hand, that of the Parish Priest presenting to the Pastoral Council decisions already made, or without the required information beforehand, or convoking it seldom only pro forma; on the other hand, that of the Council in which the Parish Priest is only one of the members, deprived de facto of his role as pastor and leader of the community[172].

---

[169] Cf. C.I.C. can. 536 §2.

[170] Cf. Ibid., can. 212 §3.

[171] Ibid., can. 536 §2.

[172] Cf. *The Priest, Pastor and Leader of the Parish Community*, n. 26: *Enchiridion Vaticanum* 21 (2002), 843.

114. Finally, it is considered fitting that, as far as possible, the Pastoral Council should consist for the most part of those who have effective responsibility in the pastoral life of the Parish, or who are concretely engaged in it, in order to avoid the meetings becoming an exchange of abstract ideas that do not take into account the real life of the community, with its resources and problems.

X. C. OTHER FORMS OF CO-RESPONSIBILITY IN PASTORAL CARE

115. When a community of the faithful is not able to be erected as a Parish or quasi-Parish[173], the diocesan Bishop, after having heard the Presbyteral Council[174], is to provide for their pastoral care in another way[175], weighing, for example, the possibility of establishing pastoral centres, dependent on the local Parish, as "mission stations" to promote evangelisation and charity. In these cases, it is necessary to furnish these pastoral centres with a suitable Church or oratory[176] and to create diocesan norms in reference to their activities, in such a way that they may be coordinated and complementary with respect to those of the Parish.

116. Centres thus defined, that in some Dioceses are called a "diaconia", may be entrusted — where possible — to a Parochial Vicar, or, in a particular way, to one or more permanent deacons, who would have responsibility for them and administrate them, together with the centre's families, under the responsibility of the Parish Priest.

117. These centres can become missionary outposts and instruments of proximity, especially in Parishes with an extensive territory, in a way that ensures moments of prayer

---

[173] Cf. C.I.C. can. 516 §1.
[174] Cf. Ibid., can. 515 §2.
[175] Cf. Ibid., can. 516 § 2.
[176] Cf. Ibid., cann. 1214, 1223 and 1225.

and Eucharistic adoration, catechesis and other activities for the benefit of the faithful. In a particular way, such missions could extend those activities relative to charity to the poor and needy and the care of the sick, enlisting the collaboration of religious and laity, and all persons of good will.

XI. OFFERINGS FOR THE
CELEBRATION OF THE SACRAMENTS

118. A topic connected to the life of Parishes and their evangelising mission, is that of offerings given for the celebration of Holy Mass, destined for the priest celebrant, and of other Sacraments, that belong instead to the Parish[177]. This means that an offering, by its very nature, must be a free act on the part of the one offering, left to one's conscience and sense of ecclesial responsibility, not a "price to pay" or a "fee to exact", as if dealing with a sort of "tax on the Sacraments". In fact, with the offering for Holy Mass, "The Christian faithful [...] contribute to the good of the Church and [...] share its concern to support its ministers and works"[178].

119. As a result, the importance of sensitising the faithful is shown, so that they contribute voluntarily to the needs of the Parish, which are "their needs", for which it is good that they learn spontaneously to take responsibility, especially in those countries where the offerings for Holy Mass remain the only source of income for priests and also the only resource for evangelisation.

120. This sensitisation will only proceed as far as the priests, for their part, offer virtuous examples in their use of money, whether it be that of a sober lifestyle, without excess on a personal level, or that of a transparent management of Parish goods. Good administration is measured not by "projects" of the Parish Priest or of a small group of persons, projects that are good but abstract, but by the real needs of the faithful, especially the poor and needy.

---

[177] Cf. Ibid., cann. 848 and 1264, 2° and cann. 945-958; cf. also Congregation for the Clergy, Decree *Mos iugiter* (22nd February 1991), approved *in forma specifica* by John Paul II: *Enchiridion Vaticanum* 13 (1991-1993), 6-28.

[178] C.I.C. can. 946.

121. In any event, "It is recommended earnestly to priests that they celebrate Mass for the intention of the Christian faithful, especially the needy, even if they have not received an offering"[179].

Among the recommended instruments for reaching this goal, one might think of receiving offerings in an anonymous way, so that everyone feels free to donate what they can, or what they think is just, without feeling an obligation to respond to an expectation or a price.

---

[179] Ibid., can. 945 §2.

CONCLUSION

122. Recalling the ecclesiology of the Second Vatican Council in the light of recent Magisterium, and considering the social contexts that are profoundly changed, the present Instruction is intended to focus the topic of renewal of the Parish in a missionary sense.

While it remains an indispensable institution to encounter Christ and to have a living relationship with him and with our brothers and sisters in the faith, it is likewise true that the Parish must constantly face changes taking place in today's culture and in the existential reality of persons, in order to explore creatively new ways and methods that allow it to be at the height of its primary function, that is, being a force of evangelisation.

123. As a consequence, pastoral activity needs to go beyond merely the territorial limits of the Parish, to make ecclesial communion more clearly transparent by means of the synergy between ministers and diverse charisms, structuring itself as a "pastoral care for all", at the service of the Diocese and of its mission.

This means a pastoral activity that, through an effective and vibrant collaboration between priests, deacons, religious and laity, as well as among different Parish communities of an area or region, occupies itself with identifying together the questions, difficulties and challenges germane to evangelisation, seeking to integrate ways, methods, proposals and means suitable to confront them. Such a common missionary project may be elaborated and realised in relation to social and territorial contexts, that is, in communities that are neighbouring or united by the same socio-cultural conditions, or in reference to related pastoral fields, for example, in a group for the necessary coordination of pastoral care for youth, universities and vocations, as already occurs in many Dioceses.

For this reason, beyond a responsible coordination of activities and structures capable of relating and collaborating among them, the pastoral care of all requires the contribution of all the baptised. In the words of Pope Francis, "When we speak of 'the people', we are not speaking about the structures of society or the Church, but about all those persons who journey, not as individuals, but as a closely-bound community of all and for all"[180].

That demands that the historical Parish institution not remain a prisoner of immobility or of a worrisome pastoral repetition, but rather, it should put into action that "outgoing dynamism" that, through collaboration among different Parish communities and a reinforced communion among clergy and laity, will orient it effectively toward an evangelising mission, the task of the entire People of God, that walks through history as the "family of God" and that, in the synergy of its diverse members, labours for the growth of the entire ecclesial body.

The present Document, therefore, besides underscoring the urgency of a this type of renewal, presents the canonical norms that establish the possibilities, the limits, the rights and the duties of pastors and the laity, so that the Parish might rediscover itself as a fundamental place of evangelical proclamation, of the celebration of the Eucharist, a place of fraternity and charity, from which Christian witness can shine for the world. The Parish, that is, "must remain a place of creativity, of relationship, of motherhood. It is there that this inventive capacity is realised; and when a parish moves forward this way, it achieves what I call 'the parish on the move' "[181].

124. Pope Francis invites us to invoke "Mary, Mother of Evangelisation", so that, "the Virgin Mother may help us to say our own 'yes', conscious of the urgent need to make the

---

[180] Francis, *Christus vivit*, n. 231.

[181] Id, Discourse in a Meeting with the Polish Bishops, Krakow (27th July 2016): AAS 108 (2016), 893.

Good News of Jesus resound in our time. May she obtain for us renewed zeal in bringing to everyone the Good News of the life that is victorious over death. May she intercede for us so that we can acquire the holy audacity needed to discover new ways to bring the gift of salvation to every man and woman"[182].

On 27th June 2020, the Holy Father approved the present Document of the Congregation for the Clergy. Rome, 29th June 2020, the Solemnity of Saints Peter and Paul.

✠ Beniamino Card. Stella
Prefect

✠ Joël Mercier   ✠ Jorge Carlos Patrón Wong
Secretary   *Secretary for Seminaries*

Monsignor Andrea Ripa
Undersecretary

---

[182] Id, Message for World Mission Sunday 2017 (4th June 2017), n. 10: AAS 109 (2017), 764.